TIM HOWARD

Marylou Morano Kjelle

Mitchell Lane
PUBLISHERS
P.O. Box 196
Hockessin, Delaware 19707
Visit us on the web: www.mitchelllane.com

Mitchell Lane

PUBLISHERS

Printing   1   2   3   4   5   6   7   8   9

A Robbie Reader Biography

Abigail Breslin	Demi Lovato	Mia Hamm
Adam Levine	Derek Rose	Miguel Cabrera
Adrian Peterson	Donovan McNabb	Miley Cyrus
Albert Einstein	Drake Bell & Josh Peck	Miranda Cosgrove
Albert Pujols	Dr. Seuss	Philo Farnsworth
Aly and AJ	Dwayne "The Rock" Johnson	Raven-Symoné
Andrew Luck		Rixton
AnnaSophia Robb	Dwyane Wade	Robert Griffin III
Ariana Grande	Dylan & Cole Sprouse	Roy Halladay
Ashley Tisdale	Emily Osment	Shaquille O'Neal
Brenda Song	Hilary Duff	Story of Harley-Davidson
Brittany Murphy	Jamie Lynn Spears	Sue Bird
Bruno Mars	Jennette McCurdy	Syd Hoff
Buster Posey	Jesse McCartney	Tiki Barber
Charles Schulz	Jimmie Johnson	Tim Howard
Chris Johnson	Joe Flacco	Tim Lincecum
Cliff Lee	Jonas Brothers	Tom Brady
Dale Earnhardt Jr.	Keke Palmer	Tony Hawk
Darius Rucker	Larry Fitzgerald	Troy Polamalu
David Archuleta	LeBron James	Victor Cruz
		Victoria Justice

Library of Congress Cataloging-in-Publication Data
Kjelle, Marylou Morano.
Tim Howard / by Marylou Morano Kjelle.
    pages cm. -- (A Robbie Reader)
Includes bibliographical references and index.
Audience: Age: 6-10.
 ISBN 978-1-68020-100-0 (library bound)
1. Howard, Tim, 1979– —Juvenile literature. 2. Soccer players—United States—Biography—Juvenile literature. I. Title.
GV942.7.H685K54 2015
796.334092—dc23
[B]
                                                                        2015003209
eBook ISBN: 978-1-68020-101-7

ABOUT THE AUTHOR: Marylou Morano Kjelle is a college English professor, freelance writer, and photojournalist who lives and works in Central New Jersey. Kjelle has written dozens of books for young readers of all ages. She holds MS and MA degrees from Rutgers University, where she also teaches writing courses. When not teaching or writing, Kjelle gardens and cooks for her family and friends, watches movies, and she reads many books. She has never played soccer, but for a few years she was a soccer mom.

PUBLISHER'S NOTE: The following story has been thoroughly researched and to the best of our knowledge represents a true story. While every possible effort has been made to ensure accuracy, the publisher will not assume liability for damages caused by inaccuracies in the data, and makes no warranty on the accuracy of the information contained herein. This story has not been authorized or endorsed by Tim Howard.

TABLE OF CONTENTS

Words in bold type can be found in the glossary.

Tim Howard was the goalkeeper for the United States when it played against Belgium in the 2014 FIFA World Cup games on July 1, 2014 in Salvador, Brazil. The United States lost the match 2-1, but Howard broke the record for the most saves in the United States World Cup history.

A Bittersweet Record

More than twenty-one million Americans watched the United States compete against the Belgians in the **FIFA World Cup** game on television on July 1, 2014. Many thousands more watched from the Arena Fonte Nova, the stadium in Salvador, Brazil where the game took place. It was the first time the US had played Belgium in a World Cup match since the first World Cup was held in 1930 and the excitement had reached a fevered pitch. The US had defeated Belgium in that **inaugural** World Cup game. Cheering fans both at home and in Brazil were counting on the US team to win the 2014 World Cup as well.

Tim Howard, the six-foot three-inch (1.91 m), two-hundred-and-five-pound (95 kg) goalkeeper for the US team knew the match with Belgium would be tough, but he believed the US team would **prevail**. Unlike other players who run up and down the field trying to steal the soccer ball, the goalkeeper mostly plays inside a penalty area. Howard's main job is to prevent the opposing team from scoring by blocking the balls they try to kick into the net. As the "keeper," Howard was determined to stop every ball the Belgium team sent his way.

Tim Howard of the United States tries his best to stop Kevin De Bruyne of Belgium from scoring in the FIFA World Cup Brazil game on July 1, 2014. Kevin De Bruyne scored.

The game was tied 0-to-0 as the teams took a break for halftime. Then, as the game entered the second half, the playing **intensified**. Tim used his hands, shoulders, feet, thighs, and legs to stop Belgium from sailing a ball inside his net. (Only the goalie can use his hands; otherwise it is illegal to use the hands or upper arm in the game.) By the end of **regulation time**, neither the US nor Belgium had scored, and the game went into **extra time.**

In the end, the US lost the match to Belgium, 2-to-1. But it was a record-breaking game for Tim. He had made fifteen **saves** in the game. That was the most saves in a single game in World Cup History.

For Tim, his World Cup record was **bittersweet**. "I would have given up that [record] in a nanosecond if we could have made it through to the **quarterfinals**," he said.

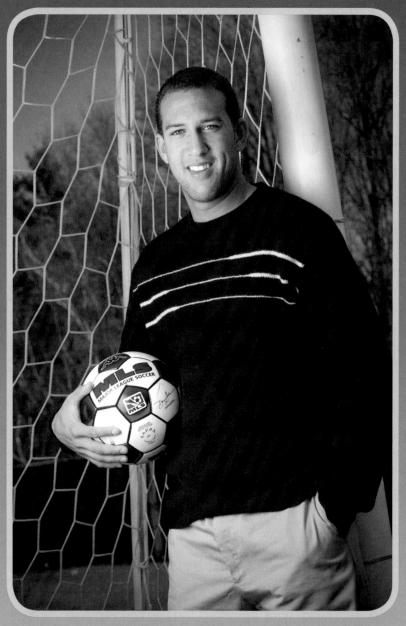

Tim was the goalie for the New York/New Jersey Metrostars in 2002, but just one year later, he was playing with Manchester United, a team that is part of the English Premier League.

A Jersey Boy

Timothy Matthew Howard was born on March 6, 1979. His father, Matthew, is an African American who drove trucks for a healthcare company. His mother, Esther, was born in Hungary. She worked for a distributor of packing containers. Howard has one older brother named Chris.

When Tim was three years old, his parents divorced. Tim and Chris were raised by their mother in a one-bedroom apartment in North Brunswick, New Jersey. Money was tight, but the two Howard brothers and their mother formed a close-knit family.

Howard didn't like school. He was a **hyperactive** child who had difficulty focusing on his lessons and he had no interest in learning. Even with extra help in summer school, he couldn't seem to earn higher grades than Cs and Ds. Esther believed that learning to concentrate on a sport might help Tim focus better on his schoolwork. She signed him up for a soccer team called the Rangers when he was about six years old. Tim wasn't good at **dribbling** or passing the ball, but he liked running and sliding, and he was fast.

"I ran past the other kids, got to the ball first, and blasted it up the field," Tim remembered.

Tim was tall for his age, so his coach made him the goalkeeper. But Tim didn't like the idea of being restricted to the penalty box. That position just didn't have enough action for him. He wanted to be able to score, not stop other players from scoring.

When Tim was in middle school, he started working with Tim Mulqueen, the goalkeeping coach of Rutgers University's men soccer team. Tim calls meeting "Coach Mulch" a life-changing experience. Mulch helped Howard move up the ranks in youth soccer. Mulch also helped Tim see that he played his best as the goalkeeper.

"I loved flying between the ball and the net, doing everything in my power to stop it," Howard said.

Not long after meeting Coach Mulch, Tim was chosen for the Olympic Development Program (ODP). The ODP identifies promising young athletes who have the **potential** to play in international competitions. Howard was also selected for the World Youth Championship team, a competition for young people much like the World Cup. As a member of that team, Tim traveled to Ecuador to attend a tournament. In addition to representing the US at games in a foreign country, Tim saw another benefit of playing on a world championship team. He was excused from school weeks at a time so that he could attend team events. In 1999, Tim was the starting goalkeeper for the World Youth Championship Games in Nigeria.

Tim Howard and Miroslav Klose, a striker for the German National Team, shake hands after Germany's 1-0 win during the 2014 FIFA World Cup match between the United States and Germany in Brazil on June 25, 2014.

As a member of both Everton and the US National Team, Tim Howard has to be at the top of his game. Training sessions like this one at Pilditch Stadium in Pretoria, South Africa in 2010 are important to him.

In the game of soccer, only the goal keeper can use his hands to make contact with the ball. In a game with Chelsea's Willian in London in February 2015, Tim Howard punched the ball, only to have it returned by Chelsea and become a goal.

Living with Tourette's Syndrome

When Tim was eleven years old, he was diagnosed with a **neurological** condition known as Tourette **Syndrome** (TS). That syndrome causes people to twitch, jerk parts of their bodies, grunt, clear their throats, yell out, and blink **involuntarily**. TS is also called the "cursing disease" because it causes some people with TS to curse uncontrollably.

At first, Tim's teachers did not realize that he had no control over those urges. They thought he was simply misbehaving. When Howard twitched and jerked in class, his classmates made fun of him.

The general public is mainly uneducated about TS. Some people consider it to be a form of mental **retardation**. Others consider it a disability.

Tim has a different way of looking at TS. He believes that it gives him the ability to see things more clearly. He also feels that TS has sharpened his other senses as well. Tim calls this the "the flip side" of TS, and he believes this fine-tuning is what makes him a good goalkeeper. For example, when it comes to penalty kicks, Howard

Diving is one of the skills necessary to be a good goalkeeper. At this game between Everton and VfL Wolfsburg, Tim Howard's dive was in vain, and VfL Wolfsburg scored a goal. The match was a Union of European Football Association (UEFA) game held in Liverpool, England on September 18, 2014.

says that his TS allows him to anticipate balls better than most keepers.

Since going public with his TS, Tim has spoken to thousands of children with the same condition. He tells them that they can do anything anyone else can do. In 2001, Howard received the Major League Soccer (MLS) "Humanitarian of the Year" award for his work with children with TS.

Javier Hernandez (#14) of Mexico kicks the ball against Tim Howard during the 2011 Confederation of North, Central American and Caribbean Association Football (CONCACAF) Gold Cup Championship at the Rose Bowl on June 25, 2011 in Pasadena, California. Mexico defeated the US team 4-2.

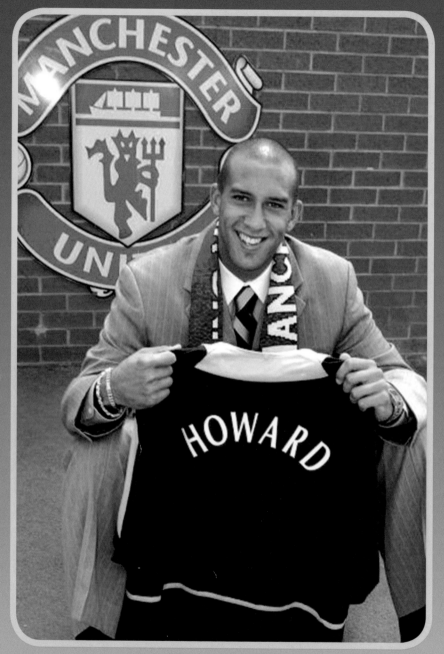

Tim Howard wore a big smile on the day he signed a contract to play for Manchester United in Manchester, England on July 15, 2003.

"Between the Ball and the Net"

Tim got his start playing soccer professionally with the New Jersey Imperials, a minor-league team. He signed on with them three months before his high school graduation. The next season he joined the New York/New Jersey MetroStars, one of the first professional soccer teams in the country. Soon after Tim turned twenty-two, he became the MetroStar's starting keeper. At the end of his first season as a MetroStar, Howard was voted MLS "Goalkeeper of the Year." He was the youngest player to have ever received that award." He was invited to play in the MLS All-Star Game. He also joined the US National Team as an **exhibition game** player.

Tim learned a lot by playing MLS in the US but he wanted the challenge of playing with a European League. In 2003, he signed on to play with England's Manchester United, the most famous soccer club team in the world and a member of the English Premier League. He ended his first season with Manchester United with the Professional Footballers' Association "Gatekeeper of the Year Award." Many consider that the most **prestigious** award for soccer in England.

Whenever he plays, Tim Howard is fully present in the game. One way he demonstrates his presence is by shouting directions to his teammates.

The pressure of playing for such a prominent team like Manchester United was overwhelming and soon Howard felt his game begin to change. "I was focusing more on avoiding mistakes than on winning the game," he said.

In the summer of 2006, Tim was loaned to Everton, a smaller team than Manchester United, but one that had been playing for more than one hundred seasons. It was a good match from the start and in February 2007, Tim became a permanent member of Everton. He has signed a contract to play with Everton until 2018. In his off season with Everton, Howard trains with the US Men's National Team. He has played in several World Cup, Gold Cup, and Confederations Cup Games.

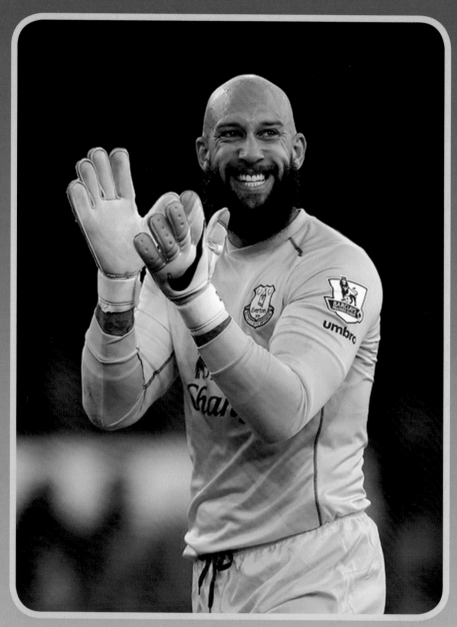

Tim Howard applauds during the Barclays Premier League match between Everton and West Ham United at Goodison Park on November 22, 2014 in Liverpool, England. Everton won 2-1 against West Ham United.

"The Keeper"

Howard is divorced and the father of Jacob and Ali. When he is not playing or training, he lives close to them in Memphis, TN.

Despite the injuries he has received, including two broken backbones, Tim has no plans to stop playing soccer. He is older than most of the other players, but that has not slowed him down. He even hopes to play in the 2018 World Cup, which will be held in Russia and Qatar.

Howard is a man of faith, which he says comes from his **paternal** grandmother. "The most important thing in my life is Christ. He's more important to me than

Striker Romelu Lukaku of Everton celebrates with Tim Howard at the end of the Barclays Premier League match between Manchester United and Everton, on December 4, 2013 in Manchester, England. Everton won this game. Howard played for Manchester United from 2003-2007.

winning or losing or whether I'm playing or not. Everything else is just a bonus," he said.

Tim continues to help others, especially children who also have TS. He works with his friend, Faith W. Rice, who is also from New Jersey, who started the New Jersey Center for Tourette Syndrome and Associated Disorders. The Center sponsors the Tim Howard Leadership Academy, which teaches life skills to teenagers fourteen to seventeen who have TS.

Representing the US National Team, Tim Howard signs autographs for fans during the World Cup training session prior to the games in the summer of 2014.

Tim Howard shows his happiness whenever Everton scores a goal.

Howard is an animal lover who doesn't believe animals should be killed for their fur. He is part of the People for the Ethical Treatment of Animals' (PETA) "Ink not Mink" Campaign. "Protecting animals is very important to me, and I think speaking out against fur is an amazing cause," he said.

Whether it is playing soccer, sharing his faith, helping children with TS, or preventing animal cruelty, Howard sets goals for himself and he keeps them.

Statistics

Year	Club(s)	GS	SB	SV	W	D	L	FC	FS	YC	RC
03/04	Manchester United	43	0	184	8	2	2	0	3	0	0
04/05	Manchester United	27	0	37	12	8	7	0	2	0	0
05/06	Manchester United	5	1	18	4	1	0	0	0	0	0
06/07	Everton/USA	40	2	225	21	13	12	2	3	1	0
07/08	Everton/USA	48	0	187	21	5	6	0	7	2	0
08/09	Everton/USA	57	0	154	8	1	2	0	5	0	0
09/10	Everton/USA	61	0	215	11	2	7	0	6	3	0
10/11	Everton/USA	49	0	139	5	1	2	3	7	3	0
11/12	Everton/USA	57	0	136	6	1	3	0	7	1	0
12/13	Everton/USA	58	0	140	9	3	3	0	11	0	0
13/14	Everton/USA	54	0	166	7	1	2	2	5	5	1
14/15	Everton/USA	34	0	112	0	0	1	1	3	2	0
Total		533	3	1713	112	38	47	8	59	17	1

Legend

GS= Goals Scored against
SB= Substitute
SV= Saves
W= Wins
D= Draws

L= Losses
FC= Fouls Committed
FS= Fouls Suffered
YC= Yellow Card
RC= Red Card

CHRONOLOGY

1979	Tim Howard is born on March 6.
1990	Howard is diagnosed with Tourette's Syndrome.
1991	Howard begins working with Coach Tim Mulqueen of Rutgers University.
1994	Howard attends the World Cup in California with the Youth National Team.
1995	Howard travels to Ecuador for the World Youth Championship Games.
1997	Howard signs on with the New Jersey Imperials, a minor league soccer team.
1998	Howard joins the New York/New Jersey MetroStars as a backup goalkeeper.
1999	Howard is the starting goalkeeper for the World Youth Championship Games in Nigeria.
2001	Howard becomes the youngest goalkeeper to receive the Major League Soccer Goalkeeper of the Year Award. He announces that he has Tourette's Syndrome and he begins encouraging children who also have TS. He receives the MLS Humanitarian of the Year award.
2003	Howard joins Manchester United, a British soccer team that is part of the Premiere League.
2006	Howard is selected as backup goalkeeper for the World Cup games held in Germany.
2007	Howard officially joins the Everton team. He plays in the Confederation of North, Central American and Caribbean Association Football (CONCACAF) Gold Cup final competition in Germany in which the US wins two-to-one over Mexico.
2009	Howard plays in the FIFA Federation Cup and he plays in the semifinal game in which the US beats Spain.
2010	Howard plays his first World Cup game.
2014	Howard makes World Cup history at a game with Brazil on July 1. The Tim Howard Leadership Academy opens in New Jersey.
2015	Howard is cleared to play again after suffering a calf injury in December 2014.

FIND OUT MORE

Books

Crisfield, Deborah W. *The Everything Kids' Soccer Book: Rules, techniques, and more about your favorite sport!* Holbrook, MA: Adams Media, 2009.

Doeden, Matt. *The World's Greatest Soccer Players.* North Mankato, MN: Capstone Press, 2010.

Jökulsson, Illugi. *Manchester United: The Biggest and the Best.* New York: Abbeyville Press, 2014.

Jökulsson, Illugi, *Stars of the World Cup.* New York: Abbeyville, Press, 2014.

Jökulsson, Illugi. *U.S. Men's Team: New Stars on the Field.* New York: Abbeyville Press, 2014.

On the Internet

The History of the World Cup
    http://www.historyoftheworldcup.com/
The Everton Soccer Team
    http://www.evertonfc.com/home
Official Website of the US Men's National Soccer Team
    http://www.ussoccer.com

Works Consulted

Bauder, David. "World Cup Ratings Soar for United States vs. Belgium." *The Huffington Post.* July 2, 2014. http://www.huffingtonpost.com/2014/07/02/world-cup-ratings_n_5553002.html

Begley, Ian. "Biggest fan backs Howard on big stage." *ESPN.* June 18, 2010. http://sports.espn.go.com/newyork/news/story?id=5300243

Herrera, J.L. "USA Soccer World Cup Profile: Goalkeeper Tim Howard." *CBS.* June 16, 2014. http://tampa.cbslocal.com/2014/06/16/usa-soccer-world-cup-profile-goalkeeper-tim-howard/

FIND OUT MORE

Howard, Tim. *The Keeper: A Life of Saving Goals and Achieving Them*. NY: HarperCollins, 2014.

Lawrence, Chris. "Tim Howard: The Goalkeeper." *Campus Crusade for Christ*. http://www.cru.org/ministries-and-locations/ministries/athletes-in-action/tim-howard-the-keeper.htm

Puckett, Jessica. "US Soccer Star Tim Howard Wants to Play in 2018 World Cup." *abc News*. December 28, 2014. http://abcnews.go.com/blogs/politics/2014/12/us-soccer-star-tim-howard-wants-to-play-in-2018-world-cup/

"Tim Howard." *Beyond the Ultimate*. 2012. http://www.beyondtheultimate.org/athletes/Tim-Howard.aspx

"Tim Howard." *Everton Football Club*. www.evertonfc.com/players/t/th/tim-howard

"USA Trying To Reach World Cup Quarters For 1st Time Since 2002." *CBS News*. July 1, 2014. newyork.cbslocal.com/2014/07/01/usa-trying-to-reach-world-cup-quarters-for-1st-time-since-2002/

Whiteside, Kelly. "Tim Howard bares tattoos for PETA 'Ink, Not Mink' campaign." *USA Today*. May 6, 2014. http://ftw.usatoday.com/2014/05/tim-howard-peta

GLOSSARY

bittersweet (bit-ter-SWEET)–both painful and pleasant

dribble (DRIB-ul) –to move the ball along the court with short kicks

exhibition game (ek-suh-BISH-en geym)–a game with no influence in ranking

extra time (EK-struh tym)–time added to the end of a match to replace time taken away because of injury or other reason

FIFA (FI-fa) –Fédération Internationale de Football Association: the international federation of football (known as soccer in the US)

hyperactive (HY-per-AK-tiv)–unusually active

inaugural (in-OGYER-el)–marking the start of something new

intensify (in-TEN-si-fy)–to become stronger, as in energy or feeling

involuntary (in-VOL-un-ter-ee)–not wanting or meaning to do something

neurological (noo-ROL-ah-gi-cal)–having to do with the nervous system in the body

paternal (pa-TUR-nl)–having to do with a father

potential (pe-TEN-shel)–having possibility

prestigious (press-TEE-gis)–honored; influence that comes from success or achievement

prevail (pree-VEYL)–to be proven superior in power or influence

restrict (ri-STRIKT)–to be kept within limits

quarterfinals (kwar-TER-fyn-als)–one of four games played between eight teams in a competition; the winners of quarterfinal games make it into semifinals

regulation time (REG-yoo-lay-shun tym)–a regular ninety-minute game

retardation (ree-TAR-day-shun)–slowed or limited in some way

syndrome (SIN-drom)–a group of symptoms that appear together that signify a specific disease

World Cup (world kup)–an international soccer tournament championship held every four years

INDEX